ATTACK
OF THE

BookLife
freedom
Readers

FUNGI

By
William Anthony

BookLife
PUBLISHING

©2022
BookLife Publishing Ltd.
King's Lynn
Norfolk, PE30 4LS

ISBN: 978-1-80155-126-7

Written by:
William Anthony

Edited by:
Madeline Tyler

Designed by:
Amy Li

PHOTO CREDITS

All images courtesy of Shutterstock.com With thanks to Getty Images, Thinkstock Photo and iStockphoto.

Used throughout (including cover) – chekart (background), Sonechko57 (slime), VectorShow (microbe characters), Alena Ohneva (vector microbes), Olga_C (circle image frame).
Used throughout (excluding cover) – Photo Melon (clipboard), Lorelyn Medina (scientist characters). P4–5 – Imagerist, Naeblys, p6–7 – ASDF_MEDIA, Peeradach R, p8–9 – svtdesign, antpkr, ranjith ravindran, p10–11 – pornpan chaiu-dom, MaryValery, p12–13 – Marcel Jancovic, Dermatology11f, Real Illusion, p14–15 – What's My Name, nobeastsofierce, VectorShow, p16–17 – Arit FongFung, MTPhoto_Life, p18–19 – MaryAnne Campbell, Svineyard, p20–21 – pinkeyes, wavebreakmedia, p22–23 – didesigns021, Africa Studio.

CONTENTS

BAD THINGS COME IN
SMALL PACKAGES

Imagine the smallest thing you can. Now try to imagine something that is so small that you cannot even see it. This is how small microorganisms are. Micro means tiny, and organism means a living thing.

Microorganisms are sometimes called microbes, and they are everywhere. They are on the ground, in the air and in our water. They are even on our skin and inside our bodies.

5

FOUL FUNGI

Fungi are a type of microorganism. They are alive and some are too small to see. Some fungi are much bigger, such as toadstools.

TOADSTOOL

Fungi cannot make their own food. Instead, they break down dead plants and animals, or feed off living ones.

TRICKY WORDS

FUNGUS = singular (one fungus)
FUNGI = plural (many fungi)
FUNGAL = to do with a fungus or many fungi

Some fungi can be good. Yeast is a fungus that we use to make our bread rise. Other fungi live safely in our bodies.

Some fungi are not as good for us. Some can lead to an infection, make us itch, give us rashes and even be poisonous to eat. When something is poisonous, it means that it is dangerous or deadly to eat.

FUNGAL INFECTION

ATHLETE'S FOOT

Athlete's foot is an infection. It is caused by a fungus growing in warm, moist areas of the feet.

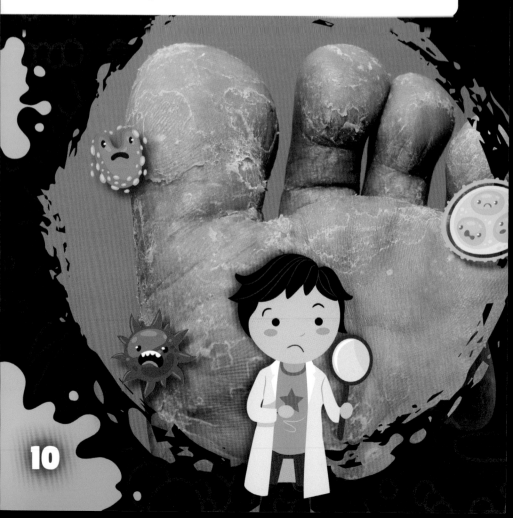

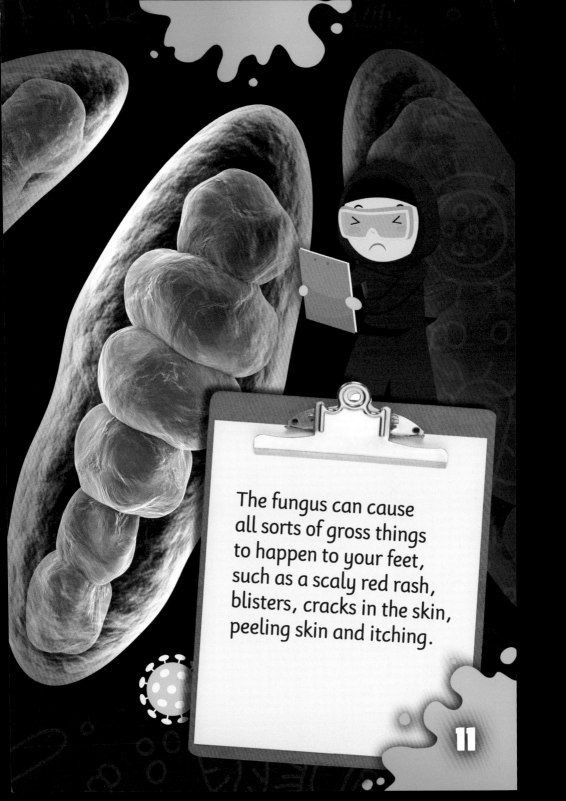

The fungus can cause all sorts of gross things to happen to your feet, such as a scaly red rash, blisters, cracks in the skin, peeling skin and itching.

RINGWORM

Ringworm is caused by the same fungus that causes athlete's foot. The fungus can live anywhere on the body, such as the hair, skin and nails. It can be spread from person to person.

Ringworm can cause lots of different things to happen to our bodies, such as ring-shaped red marks, itching, scaly skin and a spreading rash.

ZOMBIE-ANT
FUNGUS

Other animals are affected by fungi too. There is a type of fungus that can turn ants into zombies.

The fungus takes over the ant's whole body and controls it. It makes the ant walk to a leaf or a branch where the fungus can feed and grow.

JOCK ITCH

Fungi can reach everywhere on the human body. They grow best in warm places on the body. Jock itch is a fungal infection that can grow in your groin or between your bum cheeks.

Jock itch can cause redness, itching, burning feelings, a rash and dry, peeling skin.

HONEY FUNGUS

Fungi don't just invade animals. Plants can come under attack too. Some trees have to battle with honey fungus.

Honey fungus attacks the roots of a tree in order to kill it. It then feeds off the dead tree.

19

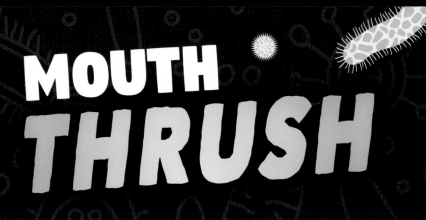

MOUTH THRUSH

A fungus called Candida is normally harmless to humans. However, it can cause an infection in your mouth called thrush.

CANDIDA

Mouth thrush can be spotted quite easily. The fungus can cause white spots, cracks in the corners of the mouth, pain and difficulty eating. It can also make things taste differently to normal.

21

FIGHTING BACK

There are lots of ways that we can fight back against fungi. We can take tablets, use creams and even have injections where medicine is put into our bodies by using a tube with a special needle at the end.

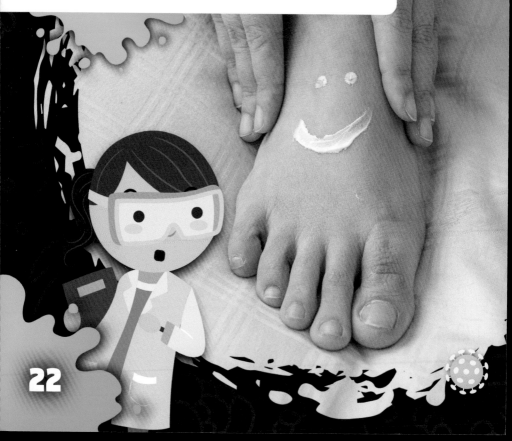

Tablets, creams and injections can kill off the fungus or stop it from growing and getting bigger. The fight back against fungi has begun!

23

QUESTIONS

1: What is yeast used for?

2: Can you name one thing that athlete's foot causes?

3: Which part of a tree does honey fungus attack?
   a) Roots
   b) Leaves
   c) Fruit

4: Apart from yeast, can you think of any other fungi that are good for us?

5: Can you think of any medicine you have had to take to fight off fungi? How did it make you feel?

BookLife
freedom
Readers